KING ALFRED

CAN YOU HEAR ME AT THE BACK?

For Peter Barkworth

Brian Clark

CAN YOU HEAR ME AT THE BACK?

AMBER LANE PRESS

All rights whatsoever in this play are strictly reserved and
application for professional performance should be made
before rehearsal to:
Judy Daish Associates,
Globe Theatre,
Shaftesbury Avenue,
London W1V 7AA.

Application for amateur performance should be made to:
Samuel French Ltd.,
26 Southampton Street,
London WC2E 7JE.

No performance may be given unless a licence has been
obtained.

First published in 1979 by
Amber Lane Productions Ltd.,
Amber Lane Farmhouse,
The Slack,
Ashover, Derbyshire S45 0EB.

Printed in Great Britain by
A. Wheaton & Co. Ltd., Exeter.

Typesetting and make-up by
Computerset (Phototypesetting) Ltd., Oxford.

Copyright © Brian Clark, 1979
ISBN 0 906399 07 6

Can You Hear Me at the Back? received its world premiere at the Piccadilly Theatre, London on 23 May, 1979. It was directed by Barry Davis and designed by Carmen Dillon, with the following cast:

PHILIP TURNER	Peter Barkworth
SARAH TURNER	Hannah Gordon
COLIN TURNER	Michael Maloney
JACK HARTNOLL	Edward Hardwicke
MARGERY HARTNOLL	Stephanie Beacham

Characters

PHILIP TURNER:	45, Chief Architect, Feltonly New Town
SARAH TURNER:	41, Philip's wife. A doctor
COLIN TURNER:	17, Philip's son
JACK HARTNOLL:	43, Headmaster, Feltonly Comprehensive School
MARGERY HARTNOLL:	39, Jack's wife. A dress designer

ACT ONE

A spot downstage on PHILIP.

PHILIP: Can you hear me at the back ...? Good ... Well now ... It seemed a good idea to us at the Development Corporation to call this town meeting to ... review progress, if you like, to see where we've got to — and to look forward to where we're going. It's now fifteen years since that first meeting in the old village, when I introduced myself to the original inhabitants of Feltonly, to explain how we were all going to grow together into a large New Town. Well, we're more than two-thirds the way through now, and though we've all had our disappointments, the postponement of the theatre, for example, and the difficulties we've had in a period of economic recession, in persuading industry to move into the excellent industrial area we've provided — nevertheless, I think we can fairly claim that we have laid the foundations for a well-planned, balanced town that our children will be proud to grow up in.
[*Spot out.*]

[*The lights fade up to show* PHILIP *looking out of the window of the living room of a Georgian house. It is furnished in the severe Scandinavian style of the middle sixties.* SARAH, PHILIP's *wife, is leafing through a sheaf of papers on her lap.*]

PHILIP: Sometimes, I think architecture is the art of spoiling fields.

9

SARAH: It's not your fault. You never wanted it to be like that.

PHILIP: So what? The thing that really worries me is that I don't know one person who could stand here, look at that view, and say: "That's entirely what I wanted".

SARAH: I should think not.

PHILIP: Then how did it happen? Nobody wanted it. We spent years, thinking, drawing plans, listening to experts, visiting Scandinavia, and in the end, we built that.

SARAH: But you weren't given a free hand.

PHILIP: You think it would be better if we had?

SARAH: You're always complaining about economy cuts, government interference, new regulations . . .

PHILIP: Yes, I know . . . and if we hadn't had all those, would it have been better?

SARAH: Of course.

PHILIP: I wonder. If you're going to build dwelling units for a population instead of homes for families . . .

SARAH: You're depressed.

PHILIP: With such penetrative diagnostic skill, you should have been a psychiatrist.

SARAH: It's no good taking it out on me. What on earth's the matter with you! For days . . .

PHILIP: Oh, I don't know. It's been growing for months, but it came to a head at the meeting last night. Do you think those people really believed what I said? Did they believe *I* believed what I said? Or did they just sit there *wanting* to believe that we had all made a sensible decision to uproot ourselves and play at shepherds and shepherdesses in a twentieth-century Arcadia.

[*Fade.*]

[*Sound of a school singing the last verse of* The King of Love my Shepherd is.]

[*Spot on* JACK HARTNOLL, *the headmaster, singing lustily. The hymn ends. Sound of coughing and shuffling.*]

JACK: All right, settle down. I heard that, Jones. Come and see me after assembly ... As you know, we are celebrating the fifteenth anniversary of the designation of Feltonly as a New Town. It's an interesting verb, 'to designate'. It is one of those words which indicates the humanness of human beings. The verb 'to fight' can apply to all life-forms — lions, snakes, sparrows, perhaps protozoa, or even dandelions — as they engage in the struggle for survival. But only man can design, designate. It comes from a Latin word *designare*, meaning 'to mark out, trace out, denote by some indication, to contrive, to devise'. It is the first stage of making a complete plan. And this activity marks us off from the rest of creation — and ennobles the species. It means that we are not the creatures of our environment, we are not thistle-down to be blown hither and thither by the impersonal, random wind. We can make our own destiny; we can seize opportunity; we can control — to a very large extent — what happens to us. I hope we will see our town's celebration as an event that marks for us our privilege of joining in an enterprise designed by caring men to make a healthier, more creative life for all the town's inhabitants ... And now some details of the school's plans for the week. There will be the junior sports day tomorrow, and I know many of you sixth-formers are helping to organise that. Thank you. On Wednesday we have the school music concert. And, by the way, this will be the first public appearance of the school string orchestra, and I am sure we are all well aware of how hard they have been practising. On Friday after-

11

noon Mr Turner, the town's architect, is coming to talk to the sixth form about the building of the town. I'm sure we're all grateful to Colin Turner for bringing pressure to bear on his father to come along.

[*The school chuckles.*]

[*Fade.*]

[*Fade up on* PHILIP. *He is at a drawing board.* SARAH *is still making notes on the sheaf of papers.*]

PHILIP: Then there's that wretched lecture to the sixth form . . .

SARAH: You'll enjoy it.

PHILIP: You must be joking . . . Can you imagine some of the questions Colin and his mates will ask . . . ? "Mr Turner, bearing in mind that the revolutionary proletariat will be establishing a New Town Soviet to set the people free, why haven't you provided a prison so we can lock up deviationist reactionaries?"

SARAH: Come on, they're not stupid . . . it's their youth . . . it's natural . . . they want change.

PHILIP: Who doesn't? The only thing that worries me is that they know *exactly* what change they want.

SARAH: And you'd rather they were confused like you?

PHILIP: Yes. Don't knock it. I've used a lot of effort to achieve this confusion.

SARAH: And very helpful it is!

PHILIP: Yes!

SARAH: It wouldn't help me. Can you imagine what would happen to my practice if I showed any doubt to my patients?

PHILIP: You'd be surprised. Do you remember old Jenkins?

SARAH: That randy old goat!

12

PHILIP: That was therapeutic. Old ladies used to hobble into his surgery, and within a couple of minutes they were skipping around the table to avoid being groped . . . anyway, he looked at a rash I had on my arm once, and with great seriousness, said . . . "Ah! That's a C.K. rash." I asked him what that was. "Christ knows!" he said. It was very comforting.

SARAH: I'd rather he knew.

PHILIP: So would I, but if he doesn't, I'd rather he told me. I don't mind doctors *pretending* to be infallible, but what if they start believing their image! Then we are in trouble.

SARAH: And I'm going to be in trouble if I don't get down to the school.

PHILIP: A medical inspection?

SARAH: No . . . it's the family planning lecture . . .
[*She takes a bag and begins to take out contraceptive devices, ticking them off on a check-list in a little black book.* PHILIP *watches.*]
Durex . . . Dutch Cap . . . Pessaries . . . Pills . . . Douche . . . Coil . . . Foam . . .

PHILIP: An elastic band?

SARAH: An elas—? Oh!
[*She repacks her bag.*]

PHILIP: What about things you can't put in your little black bag?
[SARAH *looks at him questioningly.*]
What about passion, joy, spontaneity?

SARAH: I deal with those too. All this is to make sure passion, joy and spontaneity doesn't become regret, guilt and misery . . . Aren't you going back to work this morning?

PHILIP: No, I'm taking it off. I want to finish that conversion job for Jim.

SARAH: You've been at it all weekend.

13

PHILIP: It's about finished, really.

SARAH: I should have thought you had enough of plans in the week without working on private jobs at home at weekends.

PHILIP: In the week I supervise a sewage scheme for Neighbourhood Block F/106. At the weekend I enjoy myself by fiddling with a seventeenth-century farmhouse or an eighteenth-century windmill conversion. I have to con myself I still have some taste.

SARAH: . . . If you don't believe in your work, why do you go on doing it?

PHILIP: Habit, I suppose.

SARAH: That's not a good enough reason.

PHILIP: If we're honest, it's the motive for most human activity — work, play . . . marriage.

SARAH: . . . I'd prefer to think of us as on a higher level than nail-biting or smoking . . .

PHILIP: I didn't say a bad habit . . .

SARAH: If marriage is just a habit, it's bad by definition.

PHILIP: . . . Yes, I suppose so . . .

SARAH: Philip . . . it's not just the town you're dissatisfied with, is it . . . ? It's us too . . .

PHILIP: I don't know . . .

SARAH: If you don't know, then you *are* dissatisfied. Marriage isn't something you can be uncertain about. If it isn't positive, it's negative.

PHILIP: For God's sake, Sarah, stop being so certain. A battery doesn't *have* to be positive *or* negative, it can be just flat.

SARAH: And that's how you think of us — flat, no charge.

PHILIP: I wasn't aware of thinking of us at all . . . I was thinking of the town.

> [SARAH *looks at him, then picks up her bag and goes out.* PHILIP *watches her go and then slowly picks up his pencil and tee*

14

*square and draws a couple of lines on the
plan. He stands back to look at it, then
reaches for the handset of a dictaphone near
the board. He switches it on.*]

Joan. A letter to Mr James Harvey. The address is in
the files. 'Dear Jim, Here's the sketch plan I've
worked out. Perhaps you could have a look at it and
we'll meet for a chat. This solution is by no means
the only one possible, so if you're not happy, please
say so . . . The great thing about an old farmhouse
like yours is the way it's grown over the years. When
they wanted a dairy, or another bedroom, they just
added it on. This does make for conversion
problems, in that many of the internal walls are two
feet of solid stone. But, we do have scope. It's a
generous building. It's not stretched so tight that if
you pull one corner a great tear appears thirty feet
away. The building can go on growing and
changing, and live with the people who are at
present living with it. When you and Vicky have
looked at the plans, give me a ring, and we'll chat.
Best wishes, etc.'

[*Fade.*]

[*Spot on* COLIN. *He is talking from notes.*]

COLIN: . . . When Mr Hartnoll asked me to give this paper
for the General Studies Seminar, I wondered what I
could possibly say about the New Town that hasn't
already been said *ad nauseam* — which, for the
illiterates in the Science Sixth, means 'to the point of
sickness'. Then I began to see it doesn't really matter
what I say because this General Studies lesson is like
the School Council or like the New Town Council,
even like Parliament itself, it's just a talking shop. It
doesn't matter what you say; the only point of it is

that people talk in these institutions and con themselves into believing that what they say, what they want, matters; that somebody is listening to them. And the truth is, of course, that no-one *is* listening. We have to learn to stop talking about problems and to solve them. The country has lost its way. It is a dead fish, floating on a backwater of the dialectical stream of history, and the only way to help is not to reform it — to make it go faster in the wrong direction — but to change direction. The capitalist impetus has died. You don't reform corpses, you bury them, and talking shops, from this General Studies Seminar to the High Court of Parliament, merely distracts us from the only necessary action. Revolution.

    [Fade.]

    [Fade up on PHILIP. *He is at his drawing board.* MARGERY *comes into the room.]*

MARGERY: Hello.

PHILIP: Hello Margery.

MARGERY: Is Sarah in?

PHILIP: No, she has gone to the school. She is giving a lecture.

MARGERY: Sorry to disturb you.

PHILIP: It's all right. I'm just finishing.

    *[*MARGERY *looks over the board.]*

MARGERY: What are you doing?

PHILIP: A private job. Conversion, for a friend . . . a farmhouse in Dorset.

MARGERY: Very nice.

    [She leans over the board. Her dress has a low neckline.]

PHILIP: Steady on. If you lean like that, your frontage will finish up in my bedroom.

16

MARGERY: And wouldn't you enjoy that?

PHILIP: At the time, almost certainly. But I'd rather not live next door to my mistress.

MARGERY: You don't want to spit on your own doorstep, is that it?

PHILIP: Something like that.

MARGERY: So, we stick to a bit of slap and tickle at parties?

PHILIP: Are you propositioning me?

MARGERY: Yes.

PHILIP: And what about Jack . . . and Sarah?

MARGERY: Jack fancies Sarah, I'm sure of it.

PHILIP: And so we bring this New Town paradise to its apotheosis. A wife-swop on Saturday nights.

MARGERY: We could be really daring and do it on Mondays.

> [PHILIP *leans over to her and reaches for the zip of her dress. It goes right down to her waist. Looking at her all the time, he slowly unzips her. She looks back at him and does not move.*]

. . . Yes, Philip. I'm serious.

> [PHILIP *does not move for a moment. Then he quickly zips her up again, kisses her lightly and walks away.*]

PHILIP: Sorry, Margery . . . not now . . . I'll think about it . . . but it's not the answer, is it?

MARGERY: Depends on the question.

PHILIP: And that depends on the asker of the question.

MARGERY: No, it's always the same question. How to stop being bored.

PHILIP: But the form of the question changes. Colin would say: "How can we act to promote the dialectical process of history?" Sarah would say : "How can we stop everyone smoking, get them to walk a mile a day, stop eating polyunsaturated fats and all live to be two hundred and fifty-eight?"

MARGERY: And what about me?

PHILIP: You are more honest than most, and you asked the question straight out, but in your role as a fashion designer, you probably ask yourself how you can anticipate what everyone will want to wear in six months so you can draw it, and then have everyone say you invented it . . . I'm sorry that seems a bit cruel . . .

MARGERY: No . . . it's pretty accurate, I'd say. And now, you.

PHILIP: Ah . . . ! That's difficult. To be sarcastic about one's self sounds like praise.

MARGERY: Then, tell me straight. What do you want?

PHILIP: . . . The impossible. A planned spontaneity. I want to be able to . . . crap wherever I feel like it, but I also want to be over a loo at the same time, and the loo to meet the beginning of the sewer.

MARGERY: That sounds fairly easy to manage.

PHILIP: But you haven't sweated for months over a sewage level layout for a whole town.

MARGERY: And in terms of us, you'd like to leap into bed spontaneously with me, having carefully planned that Sarah and Jack are away for the night.

PHILIP: I conceded at the beginning, it was impossible.

MARGERY: You forget about my skill in anticipating what people want and planning to have it spring spontaneously out of the air.

[*Fade.*]

JACK: [*off*] Just one minute, Jones . . .

[*Spot on* JACK.]

'Give masochists a fair crack of the whip.' If you think that's funny, Jones, I don't. I know that when we were dealing with Pompeii I dwelt on how much the Pompeian graffiti helped us to understand the life of the common people, but I did not intend you to enlighten future generations with your literary creations on the lavatory wall. And when I used the word 'common' I did not mean pornographic. And I know you're Welsh, Jones, but that word is not spelt with two f's. Now as a punishment I want you to write out the verb *graffito* fifty times . . . not on the wall, you stupid boy!

[*Fade.*]

[*Fade up on* PHILIP *and* MARGERY.]

PHILIP: When you design a dress, if it doesn't look right, you can burn it. It's only a couple of hundred at most . . . What can I do about a town?

MARGERY: You're exaggerating.

PHILIP: No . . . and I'll tell you something that's even worse. It's not that I failed at something but I failed to see at the beginning that what I was trying to do was absurd. To fail at a difficult job is acceptable, to attempt an impossible one is stupid.

MARGERY: Impossible or not, the job had to be done. Millions of people needed houses.

PHILIP: They didn't need those houses. God almighty, look at them. They don't make a town. We planned it on the principle that *everyone* would have a car. Well, they don't. And if they did, they won't be able to afford the petrol in a few years' time. It was just one of our arrogant long-term decisions affecting tens of thousands of people for a hundred years. It wasn't organic growth, just inorganic accretion. Piles and piles of bricks.

MARGERY: Words, Philip. Just words. Just because something's 'organic' doesn't make it good. Cancer is 'organic' . . . and the shanty towns of Johannesburg are 'organic' spontaneous towns.

PHILIP: . . . But not a planned spontaneity . . . Do you remember the beginning of the new towns?

MARGERY: After the War, 1940 . . .

PHILIP: 1947 ... the Labour Government, the Town and Country Planning Act. So we still had rationing and a cold war and all that but we had hope. Vision. We'd come through against the odds. We could do anything! I was only a boy then really, but you could feel it in the air. People cared. 'Welfare' was a term of praise, of pride, not a term of abuse. I wasn't interested in private practice, in building Tudor-bethan houses for stockbrokers. I've always been in public building; it was the exciting place to be. We were going to build towns and cities where the people could live free and happy lives. And we were so certain we *knew* how to do it. And we didn't. We blew it.

MARGERY: You're exaggerating.

PHILIP: I'm not ... I'm not! Look at it ... Don't try to tell me it's not too bad. At least let's learn. Let me tell you something. Before I came here I was with Local Authority Housing. I don't know one man who was keener than I was on high-rise development. There are tens of thousands of people all over London *now*, who are living boring and lonely and often vandalised lives, stacked up on top of each other, because I thought that a 'visually exciting environment' was more important than being able to chat to your neighbour over the garden fence.

MARGERY: But we have known that for ten years.

PHILIP: Yes, but have we learnt the real lesson? What are we doing now, that in fifteen or twenty years' time will not seem just as idiotic?

MARGERY: So now you throw in the sponge. And retreat into designing cosy little converted windmills for Sunday Supplement people ... I should not have said that.

PHILIP: You should. It was a perfect example of planned spontaneity; you'd thought it for a long time and it popped out.

MARGERY: ... What are you going to do?

PHILIP: I don't know. What do people do in a decadent civilisation?

MARGERY: The kids say you chuck the whole lot out and start again ...

PHILIP: But the trouble with the young is, they're so old-fashioned. Do you want a drink?

MARGERY: Yes.

PHILIP: You see, *we* have seen Hitler killing millions to save the Deutschmark. *We've* seen Stalin killing millions to stop the Tsars killing thousands. I just can't start being a middle-aged, middle-class, trendy revolutionary. I refuse to be young in heart if it means being infantile in brain.

MARGERY: So, you have no answer ...?

PHILIP: The only answer I can find is so ... embarrassing, I hardly dare mention it in polite society ... Love.

MARGERY: It doesn't embarrass me.

PHILIP: It does me. But I honestly can't think of any other principle or practice which does not end in anything but destruction.

MARGERY: I don't see why you should be so defensive. The idea has a good pedigree — at least two thousand years old.

PHILIP: Come on, Margery. Whatever Christ may or may not have said, the tradition of Christianity is just another bureaucracy, concerned with power, with money. When the meek come to inherit the earth, who's going to be at the front of the queue of inheritors, Ian Paisley? Mary Whitehouse? The Pope? Christianity has a bastard's pedigree; it doesn't know its father.

MARGERY: ... I love you, Philip.

PHILIP: Yes, I believe you do. But I'm not going to jump into bed with you.

MARGERY: There doesn't have to be any commitment.

PHILIP: Not formally, perhaps, but there does have to be communication. At present, I don't know what to say.

MARGERY: I understand.

PHILIP: I'm suffering from what the jargon calls a crisis of identity. And the really sickening thing about that particular piece of wooden speech is that it actually means something. I've been here, what, fifteen years. I designed that out there. Look at it, my brain-child. It's a wise child, they say, that knows his father. I'd like to say that bastard out there is no child of mine . . . but it is. If I were a painter, I could paint over my completed canvas; if I were a writer, I could put out a revised edition. But I'm an architect. My mind is projected and solidified in brick and steel and pre-stressed concrete. And, as I walk about the town, I'm walking about inside my own head. And the horrible thing is not that I don't recognise it, but that I do. And I hate it.

[SARAH *enters quickly. She senses the tension between* PHILIP *and* MARGERY.]

MARGERY: Hello, Sarah.

SARAH: Hello, Margery.

MARGERY: . . . I must be going.

[*She goes to the door. As she passes* SARAH *she stops, looks at her, smiles weakly, and impulsively kisses her lightly on the lips. A brief glance at* PHILIP, *and she is gone.*]

SARAH: . . . Has she decided she'd like to make it a threesome, then . . . ? When she finally gets you into bed?

PHILIP: . . . She's just said she loves me.

SARAH: I know that! Every time she looks at you, she has to press her knees together.

PHILIP: I know you're a doctor, but do you have to be so totally physical?

22

SARAH: Oh, I see. We're on the lofty spiritual plane, are we? That probably means you told her you loved her too, but that to consummate it would spoil it.

PHILIP: I told her I wouldn't jump into bed with her.

SARAH: Of course.

PHILIP: Why 'of course'?

SARAH: . . . Because you're a eunuch, Philip . . . No, that's not true. To use our son's charming phrase — 'a wanker'.

PHILIP: I'm glad you think I still have some seed, even though, apparently, I waste it.

SARAH: You're menopausal. You feel the juices drying up. You're frightened of jumping into bed in case you can't make it. All right, perhaps you should move on, build something big somewhere else. But you're frightened. So you fall back on your little conversion jobs. Because they can be *all* yours. You don't have to engage with anyone to build them.

PHILIP: They don't harm anybody.

SARAH: What a recommendation!

PHILIP: You sound as if you were urging me to go away, leave you.

SARAH: If that's what you want, do it. Don't use me as an excuse for inaction. As you're using this town.

PHILIP: It's not an excuse. You know damn well it hasn't worked.

SARAH: It's not perfect, but were you so arrogant that you thought it would be?

PHILIP: I wanted the people who lived in it to be happy, that's all.

SARAH: That's all! That's just as arrogant. Mind your own business, Philip. Building houses, schools, shops. If the people get sick, then they can come to the Health Centre — you've also built — and it's *my* job to make them better.

PHILIP: By giving them tranquillizers to help them cope with the environment *I* gave them.

SARAH: If that's what they need. If they lose a leg I give them a wooden one; if they have a cancer in their breast, I cut it off. I don't wash my hands of them because I can't make them perfect. I'm happy if I can make them better than they were.

PHILIP: Do you think I wouldn't be happy in those circumstances?

SARAH: Yes, I do. Have you forgotten the slums so many of these people came from, the flea-ridden, rat-infested terraces? And you're trying to tell me they're not happier than they were?

PHILIP: Oh yes, but now architects have discovered what everyone else knew all the time. It was a mistake to pull down those flea-ridden, rat-infested terraces. We should have renovated them. Can't you remember how we used to patronise the people who used to complain about losing their neighbour, their grannies? "Ho! Ho!" we used to say, "You'll soon get used to it. Get along to the Community Centres; learn to make corn dollies in the evenings." It was heartless, cruel. You call me arrogant; can't you see it's the realisation of that that's crushing me?

SARAH: Yes, but that's no improvement. Self pity is just a compound form of arrogance.

PHILIP: The terrifying thing about you is your moral certainty. You're as bad as Colin. He has a text from St Marx and All Engels to fit any problem. So have you. 'How I stopped worrying and learned to love myself by self-improving activity.'

SARAH: And you'd rather wallow in maudlin introspection.

PHILIP: I'd rather like to understand myself a little so I can know exactly what I'm foisting on people.

[*Pause.*]

SARAH: What's happening to us, Philip?

PHILIP: Growing old, perhaps ...

SARAH: No ... just growing away from each other ... The routines of our lives no longer connect.

PHILIP: Perhaps that's the trouble. Just the fact of routines, of endless actions motivated only by the previous action. Nothing happening to knock us together, or even knock us apart. Just steadily diverging lines of action.

SARAH: It doesn't have to be like that. Why don't we do something about it ... ?

PHILIP: Fall in love by an act of will? It's a contradiction of terms. You can will yourself to jump, but not to fall.

[*Cross fade to* JACK *and* MARGERY.]

JACK: He's a strange lad.

MARGERY: Who?

JACK: Colin ... In the sixth form General Studies lesson, he read a paper that was ... so ... so destructive.

MARGERY: Who did he want to destroy?

JACK: That's the problem. I don't think he knows. Oh, he's full of the Trotskyist jargon ... but he's too intelligent to swallow all that ...

MARGERY: You believe that extreme left-wingers are un-intelligent by definition, do you?

JACK: No ... not at all ... Just blocked off from relevant experience. Blinkered ... He takes after his father, of course.

MARGERY: And you think Philip is 'blocked off', 'blinkered'.

JACK: ... No ... Just that ... his mind rules his whole personality.

MARGERY: And that's a criticism?

JACK: Yes, it is.

MARGERY: Coming from a headmaster, it's a very odd one.

JACK: No it isn't. The personality isn't just mind, it's emotion, spirit, the body ...

MARGERY: A healthy mind in a healthy body makes a man healthy, wealthy and wise, if he sews a stitch in time before crossing his bridges to count his chicks.

JACK: Come on, Margery.

MARGERY: You're burbling, Jack. Just burbling. You criticise Philip, because his mind rules OK. But at least *something* is ruling, is leading, is doing ... something!

JACK: But where is it leading?

MARGERY: I don't know, I wish I were going there with him!

JACK: ... What are you saying?

MARGERY: Do I have to spell it out ...? I love Philip!

JACK: ... I see ... Have you discussed this with him?

MARGERY: I told him I loved him ... this morning.

JACK: And what are you ... going to do?

MARGERY: I'm going to do everything I can to get him to come away with me. If it's only for one night!

[JACK *makes to go out.*]

Where are you going?

JACK: To see Philip Turner.

MARGERY: If you do, I'll walk out of here now, and you won't see me again ever — whatever Philip says ...!

[*Fade.*]

[*Spot on* JACK. *He is addressing the sixth form assembly.*]

JACK: In this morning assembly I wanted to talk about courage. The word comes ultimately from the Latin through Old French and Middle English. It comes from the word for 'heart'. It was thought that the seat of bravery was in the heart. It was also the seat of love, and that is no accidental conjunction. Because to love is to be brave. It is to be open and defenceless. Christians believe that Christ showed the greatest love possible by accepting His crucifixion as an act of redemption for the sins of the world. The love turned the defeat into triumph. But those are just words. When we have to do it ourselves, accept, in love, a great blow, it requires the greatest bravery to continue to be open, receptive and not close up. The only way to achieve it is to realise that to close oneself is to complete the aggressive act, to join in an attack on oneself, attempted murder becomes suicide. We must remain open, even to those who would hurt us. That is why it is not strange that the word for bravery comes from the word for heart.

[*Fade.*]

[*Fade up on* SARAH *in her consulting room. She presses her buzzer.* MARGERY *comes in.*]

SARAH: Hello, Margery . . . I didn't know you were poorly.

MARGERY: I'm not. I've never felt better, I just wanted to talk to you . . .

SARAH: Well, I'm very busy at the moment.

MARGERY: I asked to be the last patient. If you like, I'll pretend to be ill so you'll see me.

SARAH: Oh Margery, of course I'll talk to you. I just thought it would be more comfortable at home.

MARGERY: I didn't want to be interrupted by Jack or Philip . . .

SARAH: I see . . .

MARGERY: Did Philip tell you I told him I love him?

SARAH: Yes.

MARGERY: And I asked him to go to bed with me?

SARAH: He didn't go into any details . . .

MARGERY: I wanted to tell you. Not act behind your back.

SARAH: That's . . . considerate.

MARGERY: It isn't, but still . . . What do you think?

SARAH: What do you expect me to think? I love Philip.

MARGERY: Do you?

SARAH: Yes . . . you think I don't?

MARGERY: He's very unhappy.

SARAH: I know . . . And you think I should give him a cuddle and tell him he's a clever boy and not to worry?

27

MARGERY: No. But I think I could help him.

SARAH: By taking him to bed?

MARGERY: By showing faith in him, in whatever way I can.

SARAH: Then you must do that.

MARGERY: Don't you care?

SARAH: Of course I care. I'm showing faith in him by believing that he won't act like a child by running to his mummy because someone has broken his toy.

MARGERY: You think I'm a *maternal* figure to him?

SARAH: Yes ... a very soft mother, if you want it straight from the shoulder.

MARGERY: Well I don't see it like that ...

SARAH: No, you wouldn't.

MARGERY: I do love Philip, very much.

SARAH: There's nothing I can say, either as a doctor or a wife. We'll just have to wait until Philip stops looking inside himself — and then we'll see which one of us he looks at.

> [*Cross fade to* PHILIP *and* COLIN. PHILIP *is at his drawing board.* COLIN *is flicking through a Sunday Supplement, whistling tunelessly.*]

PHILIP: How's the work going?

COLIN: 'A' Levels aren't work. They're just irrelevant, boring rubbish.

PHILIP: Perhaps someone should tell the universities; after all, it's a pity if all the academics in the country are wasting their time, when just a word or two from you could put them on the right track again.

> [COLIN *snorts at his father in contempt at the sarcasm. He flicks through the magazine again.*]

COLIN: Work is an essential, creative activity. 'A' Levels are just ... rote learning of so-called facts ... nothing to do with what's going on around us ... totally

28

unrelated to the political situation.

PHILIP: Oh, I don't know. If you're reading, say, Caesar's *Gallic Wars*, it's related to the political situation of first-century Europe.

COLIN: I dropped Latin at 'O' Levels. But, in any case, you're right. They do relate it to first-century Europe. But they should relate it to twentieth-century Europe, show how the conquest of Gaul was part of a dialectical historical process, leading us, inevitably, towards Socialism.

PHILIP: But first you have to understand first-century Rome.

COLIN: Karl Marx said he didn't want to use philosophy to understand the world, but to change it.

PHILIP: To change it intelligently involves understanding it ... I would have thought in my decadent, bourgeois, liberal way.

COLIN: That's your description, Dad, not mine ... You don't *want* to understand, do you?

[*Cross fade to* MARGERY *and* JACK.]

JACK: All right, all right, you've made your point. I'm sorry I mentioned his name.

[*The lights fade and* JACK *and* MARGERY *remain in individual spots.* JACK *is marking books and* MARGERY *is sewing. They think aloud.*]

MARGERY: [*pricking her finger*] Damn, if only that meant I could go to sleep for a hundred years and be woken up by a handsome ... Chief Architect.

JACK: 'Could try harder' ... mm ... I wonder what God is writing on my book at the moment: 'Could try harder'.

MARGERY: But Jack. Oh I am sorry I drive you away ... Why is it that whenever we speak only the cutting remarks get out ...? How can you know that I don't want to hurt you?

JACK: 'Silly mistakes spoil a good piece of work ...' right

... the morning was going so well until I had to mention Philip Turner.

MARGERY: But he can't mould me, I'm not one of his kids. I know I am not being fair, I want to be ... I'm sitting here doing this stupid sewing, watching him marking his stupid books. I could go next door and talk to Philip ...

JACK: 'Better but more effort needed.' What effort ...? What is to be done? I can't let it happen.

[JACK *makes for the door. The lights rise.*]

MARGERY: Where are you going?

JACK: Out.

[*Cross fade to* SARAH, COLIN *and* PHILIP.]

SARAH: How's this, do you think ...? [*reading from her notes*] 'So what ought we to expect from our Health Centres ...?

PHILIP: What is it you're writing?

SARAH: The article for the *Gazette* ... You know ...

PHILIP: Oh yes.

SARAH: It's the end of it ... 'So, what ought we to expect from our Health Centres? The simple answer is "health". The original idea was to move away from the negative idea that doctors were just to make sick people well again. We wanted to be more positive. We wanted them to be places where people were kept healthy. We wanted them to be centres of health education, screening, preventative medicine of all kinds. If we've failed in this, it is because we haven't had the money to provide the resources, human and technical, that this work needs. To obtain these is the priority for the future.'

PHILIP: It's very good ...

COLIN: You don't think it will stop people coming to you, do you Mum?

SARAH: Why should it?

30

COLIN: Well, somehow it seems that if you get sick, you've somehow failed the doctor, let the side down.

SARAH: Colin! It's a serious article.

COLIN: Yes, Mum.

PHILIP: He has a point, though. After all, if you got everything you wanted, prevented everything you could think of, bodies would still wear out.

SARAH: If Lister had thought like that, there'd be no antiseptics. You can only make progress if you start from the proposition that all is not perfect now.

PHILIP: I agree with you there. But the question is *how* do you make it better?

> [JACK *comes in tentatively. He is obviously upset.*] •

JACK: ... Hello ... I'm not disturbing anything, am I?

SARAH: No, come on in ... What's the matter, Jack?

JACK: ... It's hard to say, really ...

PHILIP: You look as if a drink would do you good. Colin, get some water please.

> [*He moves to a cupboard and pours out a couple of whiskies.*]

SARAH: Sit down ...

PHILIP: There you are. Thank you, Colin ... [*to* SARAH] Do you want a drink, Sarah?

SARAH: No.

> [*She nods to* COLIN *to leave. He exits.*]

PHILIP: Right then ... Cheers ...

> [*They drink.*]

Ready when you are ...

JACK: Margery is ... very ... distressed ... She said that she and ... Philip ... that she loved you ...

> [*He is close to tears.*]

PHILIP: Jack ... I think you're probably exaggerating the situation ... I've known for a long time that ... Margery felt a lot for me and I'm very fond of her. But

31

there has been no ... physical expression of this feeling and, as far as I am concerned, there aren't any plans for any.

JACK: You mean you haven't yet worked out the scale of the proposed development, or allocated resources?

PHILIP: Jack ... !

JACK: I mean, you will have an enquiry before going ahead with redeveloping my wife, won't you? I will have time to enter an objection?

PHILIP: I told you ...

JACK: 'There aren't any plans' ... You're a cold-blooded bastard.

SARAH: I don't believe, Jack, that Philip has ... tried to ... take Margery away from you ...

PHILIP: Thank you, dear.

SARAH: To be absolutely honest, that would require more guts than Philip has.

PHILIP: That's better! For one moment you came dangerously near supporting me!

JACK: Is it too much to ask that you pretend, just for a minute, to take me seriously? I know you really regard us all as objects to rearrange into witty patterns but just at this moment I don't feel like playing your game.

PHILIP: I'm sorry, Jack. Really sorry ... I don't know what to say ...

JACK: No. You wouldn't. As you manipulate the pieces to play your game, it just isn't on to have one of them move himself, argue back, is it?

PHILIP: Why do you insist on confusing me and my role. I'm the Chief Architect of this place. Inevitably, I give orders and take decisions. It's absurd to think I'm doing that all the time in my private life as well.

JACK: It's absurd that we let you do it.

PHILIP: You're a headmaster. You spend all *your* day telling

32

two thousand kids and a hundred staff what to do. You're general of a bigger army than mine.

JACK: You're wrong. The school's a cooperative venture.

PHILIP: That's the oldest con in the book. Pretending you run a cooperative allows you to bask in its successes alone — and share the responsibility for its failures. *"My* school has terrific 'A' Level success; mark you, I don't think *we've* got it quite right in the fifth form."

JACK: Hey, Philip! What do you think you're doing? I'm not here just to provide you with an opportunity to make smart-arse remarks at my expense.

PHILIP: Well, why are you here? You're welcome of course, as you always are, but if you attack me, I'll defend myself. That seems fair.

JACK: It would be if you were doing that. But you're not talking about you, you're not even talking about me. You're just using the opportunity to make smart remarks.

PHILIP: All my life, I've been plagued by people who believe that sincerity is inversely proportional to articulacy.

JACK: He's incorrigible, isn't he? In-bloody-corrigible.

PHILIP: . . . I'm unable to say anything if you're going to criticise the form instead of answering the content . . . I know you're upset, and I want to help . . . but I can't unless you talk about *you.*

SARAH: Jack . . . I'm not supporting Philip, generally, but he *is* right about that.

JACK: There's nothing much to say about me. Margery and I have . . . well . . . it's been . . . good. More than that, excellent. We're not the same sort of people, of course. Margery has . . . flair, I suppose you'd call it. I know very well that I'm a plodder. But it's worked. I've provided the stability, and Margery a lot of the excitement. Until Flash Harry here appeared, that is.

SARAH: You can't believe it's entirely one-sided, Jack?

JACK: Oh, Margery ... flirts ... I suppose you'd call it. Always has. But it's never been serious. I've never seen her ... like she was this morning.

SARAH: And how was that?

JACK: ... Wild ... and depressed at the same time.

SARAH: Margery *is* mildly ... manic depressive. Not pathologically, of course. She's not ill. But she does have an up and down sort of personality. And you have to learn to ignore the peaks on both cycles. Not ignore, exactly, but understand that in those moods, she's not her normal self.

JACK: I know that. The question is, does *he?*

PHILIP: Do you mean, do I conduct my personal relationships on the level of a consulting room? If so, the answer is no.

JACK: So, what are you going to do about it?

PHILIP: Do? Nothing! What do you want me to do? Treat Margery as if she were sick? Lay her on a couch and invite her to tell me how guilty she used to feel when she wet her knickers? I don't know, of course, but I think she would probably get the wrong idea.

JACK: It's hopeless.

PHILIP: Yes, it bloody well is. [*to* JACK] I'm not interested in playing games with Margery — yours or hers. [*to* SARAH] I'm not interested in treating people as finite problems to be solved. I'm no longer arrogant enough to think I can do it. Out there is a whole monumental disaster testifying to that.

SARAH: It always comes back to you, doesn't it? You, and how you feel, is the only yardstick you have. You're a selfish bastard.

[MARGERY *comes in during this speech.*]

MARGERY: He's not selfish enough!

SARAH: Hello, Margery!

MARGERY: [*to* PHILIP] You're not, you know. Why should you stand there being told how to run your life — and

34

everyone else's? Why don't you just tell them to bugger off?

PHILIP: Tell you too?

MARGERY: If you want to. I'm probably masochist enough to enjoy it.

PHILIP: Why can't you all get it into your heads that I don't want to be telling anyone what to do . . . ? I no longer know what it is. Make up your own minds, *then* let's talk.

[COLIN *has come in during this speech.*]

COLIN: Individualism rides again. If everybody's free to do what they like, then that's best for everybody — except the poor bloody kids pulling trucks in coal mines, that is.

SARAH: Colin, your father wasn't talking about politics.

COLIN: Oh yes he was!

PHILIP: Yes, Sarah, I was.

COLIN: That's good. At least you know you're a reactionary.

PHILIP: Oh yes, Colin. I am reacting, but I'm not a reactionary in your sense. I want change. Christ knows, I want change. I don't look back to some mythical 'good old days' when agricultural labourers were transported to Australia for wanting enough to eat, or people were herded into factories for fourteen hours a day by heartless employers. But nor do I want to transfer their power to the state.

COLIN: Power to the people.

PHILIP: Yes! But really to the *people*, not a collection of bureaucrats who claim to speak for them. The one thing I'm hoping is, the man who sparks the revolution, if it comes, won't appear quoting slogans from a little red book, as you would, Colin, or a little black book, or a green, or candy-striped book. Because if someone carrying their mind in a book-shaped carpet bag *does* win the revolution, then God help us all, because we will be arranged in lines to fit *his*

35

           typography, grouped to fit his illustrations; think to
           fit *his* quotation marks.

COLIN: And if this great individualist wins?

PHILIP: ... It could still be a bloody mess.

           [*Fade.*]

           [*Spot on* SARAH.]

SARAH: Well, as we've seen, marriage can be a terrible mess
           and I'm very conscious as a G.P. how much good
           you, as marriage counsellors, do to help couples
           facing difficulties. You've asked me along to talk
           about some of the physical causes of marital break-
           down and I hope I've dealt with some but, again as a
           G.P., I'm aware of just how often the breakdown of
           marriage causes the physical symptoms of illness I
           see in my consulting rooms. We really do have to try
           to forget the idea of mind and body as entirely
           separate. There is one entity, the human being, that
           manifests physical, mental and some would say
           spiritual qualities and the health of that body rests
           on all these aspects working together in a har-
           monious organic relationship. Perhaps the
           medieval idea of the necessity for the elements and
           humours to work together for physical, mental and
           spiritual health is not so ridiculous after all. Thank
           you.

           [*Spot out.*]

           [*Spot on* JACK. *He is holding a book.*]

JACK: Now this is a very interesting passage. Tacitus is
           telling how Agricola — anybody remember who
           Tacitus was? Jones? Well, you should do. Tacitus
           was the General who finally conquered Britain.
           Now Tacitus is telling how Agricola as a young man
           studied in Marseilles where ... "Greek refinement
           and provincial puritanism met in a happy blend".

He says how the "good sense of his mother" pre-vented his "passion for philosophy" becoming greater than befitted "a Roman and a senator". We can see how Tacitus — as the whole of Rome — was prepared to *use* Greek learning and skills — after all one of the real prestige symbols in a Roman home was the Greek slave as teacher for the children — but they were not prepared to allow this intellectualis-ing, this speculation, to destroy the authority of the ruling class. Throughout all this period the Greeks continued their progress in mathematics, astronomy, medicine and so on, but there was a brain-drain to Rome, and Rome — infinitely cruder in art and science — ruled the world. Now Jones, perhaps you could think of some modern parallels?

[*Spot out.*]

[*Fade up on* PHILIP. *He is pouring himself a drink.* COLIN *comes in.*]

COLIN: Hello, Dad. I didn't expect to see you.

PHILIP: I do live here.

COLIN: Not usually in the dinner hour.

PHILIP: I wanted to . . . finish the lecture for this afternoon.

COLIN: I thought you'd finished it days ago . . .

PHILIP: . . . Oh . . . yes . . . but I've been thinking . . .

COLIN: Steady on . . . It tends to destroy the authority of the ruling class . . . according to Mr Hartnoll.

PHILIP: Is that how you see me . . . as a member of the ruling class?

COLIN: As far as this town is concerned, you *are* the ruling class.

PHILIP: Is that how you see me . . . as a ruler?

COLIN: . . . Well . . . you know . . .

PHILIP: My God . . .

COLIN: Are you all right, Dad?

PHILIP: Yes . . .

COLIN: I mean, I could tell Mr Hartnoll . . . you . . . you aren't well enough. He could put it off . . .

PHILIP: Don't you want me to do it?

COLIN: Of course I do, but . . . if you're not well . . .

PHILIP: I am ready to give this lecture, Colin . . . as I've never been ready before . . .

> [*A projection screen is flown in.*]

PHILIP: Firstly, may I say how pleased I am to have the opportunity to open this Sixth Form Conference. *Art and the Community*, the programme says. And for once somebody has realised that the basis of the community is its environment. The houses it lives in, the schools it goes to, the shops it buys from, the halls of all sorts it meets in. Without building, there is no community. Without community, there is no art. The questions are, do buildings automatically make for community? Does a community automatically make for art? We know the answers. In both cases — no. Let's look at some buildings.

> [*He flicks his slide changer. On the screen comes a picture of a typical high rise development: tall blocks of flats, widely spaced on grass surroundings.*]

If a bright young architect, straight out of college, had seen this drawing twenty-five years ago, he would have drooled with delight. "Look," he would have said, "high density development, no sprawling over the landscape. A sense of openness, freedom. Grass and trees. And each living unit, a 'machine for living in'." Now we know he was wrong. You can stack flats one on top of the other, and the pre-stressed concrete can stand the pressure. But, until someone discovers a way of pre-stressing people, the strain breaks them down. Now, some planners may say, "That's very inconvenient of people. After all, this is a very economical solution. Why do they have to have their feet on the ground. We don't." As if we didn't know!

> [*He clicks again and there is a slide of the centre of a city, full of wide roads and office blocks.*]

The centre of a British city. Now, and as it used to be.

> [*A click: we see the centre of a medieval city.*]

I have never heard a convincing argument why it is a good thing to fill the centres of cities with office blocks. And there are dozens of reasons against. The roads are jammed twice a day. The leisure life of city centres is killed. Theatres, cafes, can't exist in the high rated area, and the people can't afford to live there. So, why does it happen? Because a very few people make a great deal of money and the rest of us are all too spineless and weak-kneed to say, "This is our city, not yours. Go away." It happens because a few people have the energy and drive to take away our community and we are too lazy to stop them. Now, to our community. I've prepared the slides with loving care. We may as well see them now they're here.

> [*A click: the town centre.*]

There. The town centre. I'm very proud of that. A study in cubes, I called it when I designed it. In fact, it's a brown study of boring boxes.

> [*A click: a multi-storey car park.*]

The car park.

> [*A click: a housing area.*]

And this is very important. A people filing cabinet. The only way of telling the contents of each file is the colour of the front door.

> [*A click: a community hall.*]

The Community Hall. You can do all sorts of things

39

here, badly. Plays, painting, music. Always knowing, of course, that if you had a real job that satisfied you, you wouldn't need the therapy.

[*A click: the factory estate.*]

Which brings us to this twentieth-century shrine. The plastics factory, the transistor assembly plant, the glossy printing works, the potato crisp factory, and the place where they make moulds to press the cases which will hold the clips that will fasten the wires forming the harness of the output side of the distributor, which is part of the ignition system that sparks the engine, which drives a car — nowhere at all worth going. So, what price Art in this community? At a rough guess: your body; your soul; your past; your future. And for this, you receive a box to live in, a box to move about in, a box to work in, a box to look into, and a box to die in. Three farces, two revivals of classical plays, ten folk concerts, a Gilbert and Sullivan, three exhibitions of Sunday paintings, a string quartet, and a damp squib on carnival night. If you think it's worth it — that's up to you. Me? I've had enough.

[PHILIP *comes forward away from the screen.*]

And I'll tell you why. I am fed up with Lego. That's what this town is — Lego Land. A group of us, all middle-class — and, incidentally, living up on the hill, in the only private estate — we draw plans, and rearrange the groups of houses and roads and schools and factories. Of course, we ask questions about your welfare, but we don't ask *you*. We ask the psychologists and sociologists at the Ministry of Housing and the County Council. We make a whole town *for* you, not *with* you. We have enormous energy at our disposal, and we use it to play toy towns, and the only thing left to the toy people to do in it to make it their own, is to squirt aerosol obscenities on the walls. There is nothing in this town that's crazy. Plenty that's stupid — but nothing that's just crazy — human, ridiculous. It hasn't grown out of the landscape, it's been plonked on it. Christopher Wren's memorial in St Paul's reads: "If you want his memorial — look around you". But he didn't want that to apply to just the church, but to the whole of London. Thank God he didn't get his way. London grew up crazily and today there is still left some of the little streets and tiny shops and theatres, and all the other absurd and uneconomic use of space that makes a real city. Even though the Lego Land builders are trying to destroy that too. Don't let them do it.

[*Spot on* MARGERY.]

MARGERY: Great, Philip. Marvellous.

[*Spot on* JACK.]

JACK: Emotional. How do you think that will help us to get the sixth form thinking positively?

[*Spot on* COLIN.]

COLIN: It was all true enough — but superficial.

[*Spot on* SARAH.]

SARAH: Self-indulgent . . . what are you going to do now?

PHILIP: . . . Resign, I suppose.

END OF ACT ONE

ACT TWO

Sounds of an office party. There is laughing and chatter. A glass is tapped. Spot on PHILIP. *He is holding a wine glass.*

PHILIP: Ladies and Gentlemen . . . too formal . . . colleagues . . . too prissy . . . friends . . . not completely accurate, but let it suffice . . . First of all, thank you very much for this . . . send-off . . . I have often left work on a Friday feeling punch-drunk — this will be the first Friday I have left work just drunk on punch. It was a complete surprise — not, you understand, that I didn't believe that my Architects' Department couldn't plan anything as ambitious as this party — but because you managed to plan and execute the party without the details being leaked to the very person who shouldn't know. So, firstly, thank you for the surprise. Secondly, you have been the most loyal and hard-working team that any chief architect has ever had. The conception of the town was mine, so the responsibility is mine. The execution was yours, and I could not have asked for better support. And so I leave . . . It is not so hard. Recently, I was thinking about an article I wanted to write for the *Architects' Review*. It occurred to me that one of the features of a New Town is the paucity of the materials that makes it. In terms of sheer bulk, a new town would weigh about . . . a tenth of an old town. There are at least two results flowing from this. In physical terms, there is much less scope for altering it organically. To change it, means, in effect, to knock things down and start again. The other effect is psychological. It feels impermanent, weightless. It is harder for the people to put down roots because the buildings themselves are so obviously resting lightly on the soil . . . And so I can more easily pull up my roots. Where I shall put them down again I do not know, but wherever it is, I shall think of you all, and wonder how on earth you are managing to complete the master plan on the miserable amount of money that's coming to you. So . . . goodbye and good luck.

[*Fade.*]

[*Fade up on* SARAH. *She is alone, thinking.* COLIN *comes in.*]

COLIN: Hi . . .

SARAH: You're very late . . .

COLIN: Sorry . . . Stayed after school . . .

SARAH: You could have let me know . . .

COLIN: I'm sorry . . . Did you leave my dinner in the oven?

SARAH: No . . . We . . . haven't eaten yet. Your father's late too.

COLIN: Oh, I see!

SARAH: What?

COLIN: Why you're so upset with *me!*

SARAH: No you don't . . . *He* rang to say he'd be late. The office laid on a farewell drink for him . . .

COLIN: Oh . . . I see . . . Are you all right, Mum?

SARAH: Yes, of course . . .

COLIN: You're not . . . You've been crying . . .

SARAH: It's all right.

COLIN: Is it Dad? Resigning and all that . . . ?

SARAH: It's nothing, Colin.

COLIN: . . . You don't mind him going away for a few weeks, do you?

44

SARAH: Of course not.

COLIN: When's he going?

SARAH: Monday, first thing. He has that talk to the History Society on Saturday afternoon, and he is reading the lesson at the Civic Service on Sunday evening.

COLIN: Oh God! Surely not. He's always said it was such a bore. This year of all years he has the perfect excuse.

SARAH: I know. But he really wants to do it for some reason.

COLIN: And when's he coming back?

SARAH: I'm not sure . . .

COLIN: . . . He *is* coming back, isn't he . . . ? You mean, you might be splitting up? Permanently?

SARAH: I don't know . . . Perhaps we'll get together again.

COLIN: Do you want to?

SARAH: I don't know, Colin. We both need time to think.

COLIN: Think . . . ? What's that mean?

SARAH: Oh Colin . . . I can't explain really. Your father's unhappy.

COLIN: With the town. That's not your fault.

SARAH: Not just with the town . . .

COLIN: With you too!

SARAH: No, it's not as simple as that . . . and it's not just your father . . . We've drifted apart . . . and we need time to think . . . to understand what's happened to us, and we're more likely to be able to do that if we're apart for a bit.

COLIN: So you want it, as well.

SARAH: . . . It seems . . . necessary.

COLIN: Who to? *You?*

SARAH: I understand why it has to be like that.

COLIN: You're hedging. Do you want him to go away?

[PHILIP *enters.*]

SARAH: Your dinner's ready . . . It's in the oven. I'll get it out.

PHILIP: There's no need to . . .

[*But she is gone.*]

Have you been upsetting your mother?

COLIN: No ... I rather think you have.

> [PHILIP *looks at him questioningly.*]

I gather you two might be splitting. That your two or three weeks' holiday might be extended indefinitely.

PHILIP: ... It could be ... We need to think ...

COLIN: If you need to think, it's all over.

PHILIP: ... Does it upset you?

COLIN: Yes ... But I'd understand.

PHILIP: That's generous, Colin. And sophisticated.

COLIN: You needn't sound surprised.

PHILIP: No. But relating to a bright eighteen-year-old is a bit like trying to make love to a mermaid. It's challenging, but you're either scraping yourself on the rocks or gasping for air in twenty fathoms of gloomy water.

COLIN: And you prefer a sitting target.

PHILIP: Ah! We're back on the rocks. No, Colin. I don't like targets at all, sitting *or* flying. I can't stand violence.

COLIN: You're amazing, Dad. You're one of the most violent men I know. You came here and you swept away a village and fifty farms, about 35 square miles, a good atom burst, and then you don't like the town you plonked in the ruins, so you'd like to level it. I happen to agree with you on both counts but don't you pretend that a meek, gentle man would do either ...

PHILIP: No ...

> [*Fade.*]

> [*Sound of a school bell.* JACK *enters. The intercom buzzes.*]

VOICE: Oh, Mr Hartnoll, Dr Turner asks if you have a moment to spare.

JACK: Dr Turner? Oh, of course. Has she finished her class today?

VOICE: Oh yes, Sir.

[SARAH *enters.*]

JACK: What a pleasant surprise . . .

SARAH: Just passing, really . . . Finished your second year personal relationships course . . . New classrooms?

JACK: Yes . . . We've only been open five years and we're overcrowded . . . We're having to put those classrooms on the tennis courts . . . Philip was furious.

SARAH: I remember . . . "How can you plan if the so-called experts who brief you can't see beyond the end of their noses?"

JACK: It's not the authority's fault really. They don't actually cause birthrate fluctuations.

SARAH: Come on, Jack. Those classrooms aren't for kids who were born in the last five years.

JACK: How was the course?

SARAH: Oh, all right . . . except the irony of the title did strike home . . . Personal Relationships — me being the expert.

JACK: Oh yes . . . Margery.

SARAH: No . . . Philip.

JACK: It's the same thing.

SARAH: I don't think so . . .

JACK: What are we going to do?

SARAH: Nothing . . . They'll make their minds up and we'll adjust.

JACK: That seems so passive.

SARAH: Is it? What do you suggest? Chaining them up? Putting them to bed without their supper . . . ? No, I don't think so.

JACK: I lie awake, wondering what I'll do if Margery leaves me . . .

SARAH: . . . Yes . . .

JACK: What would *you* do?

SARAH: If Philip left ... ? Carry on, I suppose.

JACK: ... Yes ... I envy you your strength.

SARAH: It's mostly on the outside ... A professional mask ...

JACK: I feel I ought to be offering some sort of support ... strength.

SARAH: The strong man bit ... ? I've had enough of that.

JACK: I can understand that ... Well, my weakness is available ... If you should ever need it ...

SARAH: You're not weak, Jack ... It's not weak to be flexible. Philip and Margery ... they have the weakness of cast iron.

> [*The school bell rings.*]

I had better let you get on.

JACK: Sarah ... if ... Margery does go ...

SARAH: Let's not anticipate the worst ... eh Jack?

JACK: ... No ...

SARAH: We'll be seeing you on Sunday ...

JACK: ... Oh yes ... I'm looking forward to that ...

SARAH: To Philip's farewell drink? [*not unkindly*] I'm not.

> [SARAH *exits.*]

> [*Fade.*]

> [*Fade up on* COLIN. *He is lying on his bed, learning a speech from* Lear.]

COLIN: 'Take physic, pomp;
Expose thyself to feel what wretches feel,
That thou mayst shake the superflux to them,
And show the heavens more just ...'

> [*He gives the clenched fist salute.*]

Right on Comrade King Lear.

> [*He is bored and drops the book by the side of his bed. He whistles tunelessly.*]

What are you saying, Chief Architect? Resign? You won't be able to keep your hundred assistant archi-

tects ... Ah, ingratitude, thy name is Feltonly ... I
shall go mad ...
'They went to sea in a sieve they did
In a sieve they went to sea
In spite of all their friends could say
On a winter's morn, on a stormy day
In a sieve called Feltonly.'
        [*He gives the clenched fist salute.*]
Right on Comrade Edward Lear.
        [*He smiles to himself, then whistles tune-
        lessly.*]
'*Gallia in tres partes divisa est.*' Gaul is divided into
three parts. Feltonly is divided into three neigh-
bourhood districts. Right on Comrade Caesar.
Architect is divided into two parts. *Archi-* and *-tect.*
[*imitating* JACK] It's an interesting word 'architect'.
Oh yes it is ... From the Greek *archi* meaning 'chief'
and *tectus* meaning 'builder'. Chief Builder. So chief
architect means Chief Chief Builder. Ha! Ha! The
Chief Architect himself is divided into two parts.
One who wants to build and one who doesn't want
to build. The Architect and the Archi-non-tect, or
even further, the Archi-un-tect. The chief taker-
down of buildings. It's an interesting word archi-un-
tect. Can you unbuild? You can destroy but can you
unbuild? Isn't that a contradiction in terms? 'These
whom God hath joined together ... Let no man put
asunder.' [*He slumps.*] Oh God ... !
        [*He dissolves into tears.*]

        [*Fade.*]

        [*Fade up on* SARAH *and* PHILIP.]
SARAH: Are you really going to read the lesson at the Civic
        Service?
PHILIP: Yes.

SARAH: Why?

PHILIP: Why not? It seems a fitting end.

SARAH: What are you going to read?

PHILIP: ... I'll think of something ...

SARAH: Well, I'll stay home and get ready for Jack and Margery.

[PHILIP *looks at* SARAH.]

You haven't forgotten you've asked them round for a farewell drink?

PHILIP: No, I haven't forgotten ... but what's there to get ready? It won't take long to unscrew a couple of bottles.

SARAH: I thought, some canapés, some quiche ...

PHILIP: I asked them for a drink, not to a cocktail party.

SARAH: ... It's going to be a difficult enough evening as it is, without making it completely spartan.

PHILIP: Why should it be difficult? I haven't made love to Margery; I haven't had a fight with Jack, and Colin doesn't think I'm important enough to row with.

SARAH: ... And me?

PHILIP: You've categorised me as a menopausal male that will probably settle down into increasingly quiescent senility, once I've come to terms with my failing powers.

SARAH: ... Has it ever occurred to you that you are always thinking about yourself from the viewpoint of other people?

PHILIP: It's called getting a three-dimensional view.

SARAH: Even Narcissus was satisfied with two dimensions.

PHILIP: But *he* drowned ... You are right though, but it's not just me, it's the whole country. Have you noticed that every time there's an 'Economic Crisis Special' on the telly — about three times a week — they always have to have an industrialist from Germany or a banker from Zurich — whom they introduce self-deprecatingly as a 'Gnome' — and that wouldn't matter, except he always *looks* like a gnome. Anyway, they always have a foreigner to say what he thinks of the British economy.

SARAH: That's understandable. It's the foreigners' money, after all, that keeps us going nowadays.

PHILIP: It always has. A hundred years ago we stole it from people who had nothing. At least now we have the grace to borrow it from people with a lot. *That* is real progress!

SARAH: Tell me, Philip, do you really believe the things you say, or do you just say them because they're neat, or witty?

PHILIP: ... Like a mathematician, I believe that an elegant solution is more likely to be right than a clumsy one ... I like to follow my mind.

SARAH: It leads you to strange places.

PHILIP: Isn't that better than forcing it along a muddy path?

SARAH: ... I hope Sunday night goes off without ... well, without traumas.

PHILIP: That's a negative ambition. I hope it will go off ... splendidly.

SARAH: ... You didn't answer me when I asked why the evening shouldn't be difficult for me.

PHILIP: ... No ...

SARAH: I realise of course, that you asked Jack and Margery around just so you wouldn't have to face the appalling prospect of a last evening with me.

PHILIP: Is it a last evening? You seem very sure of what we'll both decide.

SARAH: I'm very sure of what I want.

PHILIP: What's that?

SARAH: You. And I'm pretty sure of what you want as well.

PHILIP: What's that?

SARAH: The same thing. You.

[*Fade.*]

[*Fade up on* JACK *and* MARGERY, *in the school.* JACK *is counting money.*]

JACK: Well, that went well, didn't it?

MARGERY: Did it?

JACK: Must be what — £30.

MARGERY: Oh God, you're not going to count it now, are you?

JACK: Sorry. I'll do it tomorrow . . . £30 . . . That will make £480 in the swimming pool fund . . . £30 the way inflation's going, that'll buy us one tile . . . I seem to get the impression that you're not in a conversational mood tonight.

MARGERY: We've left the school now. Save me the schoolboy sarcasm.

JACK: . . . I'm sorry . . . Is there anything I can do to help? Apart from asking Philip Turner to leave Feltonly . . . I'm sorry.

MARGERY: I don't want to hurt you, but I . . . I can't help it. I love Philip . . . Look, I can't stay here now . . . I'm going up to town.

JACK: We'll both go . . .

MARGERY: No . . . I want to go alone. Don't worry. I won't do anything silly, but I don't want to be here for the next few days . . .
[*She makes to go.*]

JACK: But where will you stay?

MARGERY: I didn't say I was going to the Sahara. I said I was going to London. There are hotels . . . I'm going now.

JACK: Don't you want some things, some clothes . . . ?

MARGERY: See you next week. Jack . . . don't follow me! Leave me alone!
[*She rushes off.*]

[*Fade.*]

[*Spot on* PHILIP.]

PHILIP: Obviously, when I agreed to lead this discussion with the History Society, I didn't know this was to be one of my last civic duties in this town. I remember your secretary asking me to talk about the history of the Garden City and New Town idea. I agreed then, but you've all read accounts in the local papers of what I said at the Sixth Form Conference — and I don't really want to add anything. I did think of cancelling this talk but I decided there was something I wanted to say very much before I leave Feltonly, and the History Society is just the place to say it. Because what I wanted to talk about was the history of computers. Now some people think that computers are just big adding machines; they are essentially stupid, and quote the gar-gar principle: garbage in, garbage out. And he will say that man is in control. All he has to do if he doesn't like it, is to turn them off. The fact is, he can't; he's already handed his life over to them. Turn off the computers in the City of London and the whole economic life of the country would collapse. Turn off the radar-like defence systems and we have no defence. Take away the pocket calculators from your kids and they can hardly add up their pocket money.

[*Fade.*]

[*Fade up on* SARAH. *She is writing a letter. She signs it, picks up the paper and reads aloud.*]

SARAH: 'Dear Philip, It's strange writing to you when we share the same house but I want to talk to you and when I try it all disappears behind a cloud of words — usually yours. I suppose what I want to say is that I love you, but why don't I just say that to you instead of having to resort to a letter like an eighteenth-century heroine? Or, better still, why don't I just show you? I don't know. We have lived together so long that we are strangers. We have built our lives consciously, step by step, but somehow the steps behind us have disappeared and there is no way back to that pleasure of discovery. That wouldn't matter so much but I don't see any steps ahead. There seems to be nowhere to go, at least for me. And what I fear is that there will be some steps for you and you will go on without me. It's as though we had with our lives demonstrated that marriage is an institution and our voices echo down corridors, bouncing from the unyielding walls. In an institution there are only professional relationships. The house-mother is paid to mother, and ours has become a professional marriage. I know you think I'm cold and clinical but I want you to know that *I* know the spontaneity is gone and I want you to know I miss it as much as you. If you find some steps, please try to find room on them for me too. Yours, literally, Sarah.'

> [*She looks at the letter, thinks, then tears it up. She drops it in the waste-paper basket, and goes out.*]

[*Fade up on* PHILIP, JACK *and* COLIN.]

JACK: [*speaking from the audience*] Philip, that's much too much of an exaggeration. It's still man's mind that employs them.

PHILIP: No, Jack. Have you a reaction time in micro seconds? Because in a crunch, that's all the time you're going to have to think of a solution. Otherwise, a computer will already have made your decision for you and despatched the missile or whatever.

COLIN: If we're responding to a missile, Dad, it's all over

anyway. Most decisions we still make ourselves.

PHILIP: I don't think so. Think of the difference in reaction time between the latest IBM machine and the first computer we know about. It took three hundred years to build and for all that time it must have used up all the available surplus economic resources. But why did they build it in stone, dragging the blocks from South Wales? Why not wood? It would have worked just as well as an astronomical computer. Perhaps they believed in the future and wanted to leave something for it, a useful monument. But our computers are dedicated to extracting everything they can, *now*. How can we use up the North Sea oil in fifteen years instead of twenty? How can we cover more and more of the countryside with concrete strips. It's as though we are terrified that when we die, we'll have to leave something for our children.

JACK: In every age there are Jeremiahs crying that unless we change our ways we will be punished.

PHILIP: Yes, but have you forgotten that Jeremiah was right? But when *we* come to weep at the waters of Babylon, we shall probably find that they have been culverted.

> [*Fade.*]

> [*Fade up on* SARAH. *She is arranging some flowers on the coffee table.* PHILIP *comes in with some bottles.*]

SARAH: There's some consolation in Margery not coming. At least I don't have to worry about what the flowers look like.

PHILIP: There's no news of her?

> [COLIN *comes in with a record.*]

SARAH: I saw Jack just now. He hasn't heard anything . . . Come on, you two. We've only got a few minutes before church . . .

> [*She hurries out.* COLIN *puts a record on the turntable.*]

PHILIP: You're not going to play that, are you Colin . . . ?

COLIN: I was just getting ready to play music after the service — to calm the savage breasts.

PHILIP: I hate background music. It's a substitute for genuine atmosphere.

COLIN: . . . You're a real puritan, Dad.

PHILIP: Yes . . . I am . . . But aren't you? If the Civil War were to break out again, I can't see you rushing to the defence of the throne.

COLIN: I wasn't referring to that.

PHILIP: I know. We're both puritans, actually. Just a different vintage.

COLIN: And faction. I'm a Leveller. What are you?

PHILIP: When I look out that window, I'm a Leveller too.

> [SARAH *comes back with some canapés.*]

SARAH: Come on, you two. Look at the place.

> [PHILIP *and* COLIN *look around the immaculate room in amazement.*]

PHILIP: Why, what's wrong? It looks just like a photograph in *Ideal Home* of a trendy architect's house, circa 1965. Mostly sensible Scandinavian, with a totally absurd item or two to constitute the 'fun' element.

SARAH: You haven't finished getting out the glasses — and none of them are wiped — and Colin, clear away those magazines.

PHILIP: But Sarah, those are the 'casual' element, to show we don't actually live in a shop window . . . Christ! They're the only things that show anyone actually lives here at all.

SARAH: Oh, Philip . . .

PHILIP: All right, all right . . . Colin, you remove the human droppings there, and I'll make sure no-one catches cholera from the glasses.

[PHILIP *takes a cloth to polish the glasses.*
SARAH *goes on out to the kitchen.*]

COLIN: I'll say one thing for you, Dad. You're bloody single-minded. Once you've decided that planning's out, you lay waste everything. Even your precious room.
[PHILIP *looks around the room.*]

PHILIP: ... Yes.

COLIN: Where are you going to live when you go away for your 'think' — in a cave?

PHILIP: It's not a bad idea. Get back to the roots. It occurred to me the other day, we only started building houses at all because of the dreadful cave shortage at the time. And we haven't changed much — we just go into a piece of virgin forest, make a clearing and plonk down some houses.

COLIN: It won't change till you realise that building a town is a political act.

PHILIP: You think I don't realise that! How do you think that out there happened? By drawing lines on paper? Piling bricks on bricks? That's just the mechanical part. Of course, the town is a political act. From the Greek word *polis*, a city.
[SARAH *comes in.*]

SARAH: Well, that's that. We're ready now, I think.

PHILIP: Not quite. We haven't sterilised the teaspoons yet.

SARAH: Colin, do you have to wear those training shoes for *every* occasion?

COLIN: Mum!

PHILIP: Of course he does. It's the symbol of youth. At any moment, they're ready to run like hell.
[*Fade.*]

[*Sound of a church organ.* PHILIP *turns his drawing board round to become a lectern.*]

PHILIP: The first reading is taken from the eleventh chapter of Genesis, beginning at the first verse.

57

'And the whole earth was of one language, and of one speech. And it came to pass, as they journeyed from the east, that they found a plain in the land of Shinar; and they dwelt there. And they said one to another, Go to, let us make brick, and burn them thoroughly. And they had brick for stone, and slime had they for mortar. And they said, Go to, let us build a city and a tower, whose top may reach unto heaven; and let us make us a name, lest we be scattered abroad upon the face of the whole earth. And the Lord came down to see the city and the tower, which the children of men builded. And the Lord said, Behold, the people is one, and they have all one language; and this they begin to do: and now nothing will be restrained from them, which they have imagined to do. Go to, let us go down, and there confound their language, that they may not understand one another's speech. So the Lord scattered them abroad from thence upon the face of all the earth; and they left off to build the city.' Here endeth the first lesson.

    [*Fade.*]

    [SARAH, PHILIP, JACK *and* COLIN *come in.*]

SARAH: Come on in, Jack.

JACK: Thank you . . . I shan't stay long . . .

PHILIP: Nonsense. I've got two bottles of whisky and only enough room in my case for one.

SARAH: Let me have your coat, Jack . . .

PHILIP: Now, what will you have . . . ?

JACK: Whisky will do fine.

PHILIP: Right.

    [*He goes to the drinks.*]

JACK: So, you've left the Corporation then, Philip . . . ?

PHILIP: Yes, the last official farewell platitude has limped

from the Chairman's lips . . . the last earnest hand
has been shaken . . . and I have got over the hang-
over from the last office party . . . I have absolutely
left.

JACK: And no second thoughts?

PHILIP: No regrets, if that's what you mean . . .

JACK: It's nice to meet someone who knows what he wants.

PHILIP: I wouldn't say that, Jack . . . I just know what I don't
want . . .

JACK: And how do you feel about it, Sarah?

SARAH: It's up to Philip. He has to do his thing . . .

PHILIP: [*bringing the drinks*] There you are . . . What will
you have, Sarah?

SARAH: A martini, please . . .

COLIN: And I'll have a beer, Dad . . .

PHILIP: Right . . .

JACK: And what are you going to do now?

PHILIP: I don't know . . .

JACK: You must have some plans . . .

PHILIP: Why? For twelve years I've had plans up to here. I bet
I've used the word plan or planning, twenty times a
day, that's a hundred times a week . . . five thousand
times a year . . . that's sixty thousand 'plans'. I need a
plan like a housing authority needs another Ronan
Point.

JACK: But you have to do something . . .

PHILIP: I suppose so . . . I'll go to Scarborough.

SARAH: Scarborough?

PHILIP: Why not? I spent a day there once, when I was a
student . . . I was driving north with a girlfriend . . . I
remember showing off abominably, lecturing on
how the economic life of the town, the harbour and
promenade, and so on, had dictated the town plan
. . .

SARAH: I'm sure she was impressed . . .

59

PHILIP: No ... She was a biologist, and spent the entire day examining seaweed, lecturing me on the way the geography of the shoreline dictated its ecology. It occurs to me that, if we'd had the humility to listen to each other, we would have discovered we were giving the same lecture.

SARAH: A coincidence.

PHILIP: No ... it's always the same lecture. How what was governs what is. How what is governs what will be.

COLIN: Yes, that's what Karl Marx said: 'the dialectic'.

PHILIP: Perhaps.

JACK: Then we ought to be able to plan the future with confidence.

PHILIP: No, Jack. Because what is has a thousand possibilities. And it seems our fate to choose the most unfruitful and plump for that.

SARAH: But we needn't ...

PHILIP: No, that's why I resigned.

SARAH: ... I'm sure we haven't invited Jack for a wake ...

PHILIP: I'm sorry ...

[*He carries the drinks to* SARAH *and* COLIN.]

JACK: Well ... To the future, Philip.

COLIN: I'll drink to that.

PHILIP: I won't. To the present.

COLIN: All right ... To the present ...

[*They drink.*]

JACK: Have you decided to abandon the future then, Philip?

PHILIP: No ... I've merely decided not to pervert it.

JACK: By planning ... ?

PHILIP: If you like.

SARAH: But you *have* to plan, Philip. It's not possible to muddle through from day to day. If you want your children to be more than barely literate, you have to plan to build schools and universities; if you want to

60

      . . . cure cancer, you have to build laboratories, plan
      how to support them . . .

COLIN: I'm afraid Dad has retreated into being a middle-
      aged hippie. Next time you see him, he'll be strolling
      along the sands of Scarborough, wearing a kaftan
      and beads, giving out flowers to the deck-chair
      attendants . . .

PHILIP: I can imagine worse fates . . . but you won't be seeing
      that, Colin . . . I'm not looking for some golden age
      . . . some Arcadia . . . that's precisely what I don't
      want. I don't believe in golden ages in the past, and I
      don't trust the Utopias of the future. Stalin gilded
      with blood the young Soviet Union, to make its
      future golden.

SARAH: You can't seriously compare yourself with Stalin.

PHILIP: In a way, I can. Go into Islington now. See what
      they're building. Good little terraced houses, each
      with a little garden. That's what the people want;
      that's what they wanted in the fifties and sixties. But
      I knew so much better. Yank them out of the city.
      Bring them out to these sylvan glades, so the nymphs
      and shepherds could disport themselves amongst the
      sheep; live in tastefully grouped living units all
      provided by the New Arcadia Corporation.

SARAH: They didn't have to come.

PHILIP: Of course they had to come. They had nowhere else
      to go.

JACK: So, away with all planning! Let's live in an England
      that has ribbon development on every country road,
      a bijou residence on the top of every hill, a
      chromium hotel on the top of Scafell Pike, and
      bungalows called *Chez Nous* and *Dunromin'* all the
      way down the Cambridge Backs. There's enough
      greedy Philistines about to do all that . . .

PHILIP: Yes I know — and there's the problem . . .

> [MARGERY *walks in. She is dressed in a*
> *beautiful soft wrapover gown.*]

MARGERY: And here is another one.

JACK: Margery . . . I didn't know . . .

MARGERY: I got back an hour ago . . .

SARAH: You look lovely.

MARGERY: Thank you.

JACK: Is it a new dress?

MARGERY: You don't think I could go to London without buying a dress, do you?

> [*The phone rings.*]

PHILIP: Hello . . . It's for you Sarah. Margery, sit down.

SARAH: Dr Turner . . . Yes . . . How often . . . ? All right . . . Don't worry . . . I'll come along . . . You've informed the midwife, have you? Good. Don't worry. I'll be along shortly.

> [*She replaces the phone.*]

Damn . . . Mrs Webster in labour . . . I'm terribly sorry, I shall have to go . . .

MARGERY: She's having it at home? I thought that was a thing of the past.

SARAH: So did I. But now we have a sudden upsurge of these natural childbirth freaks . . . You know, have your baby happily at home, in between grinding your own flour and baking the bread . . .

MARGERY: It *is* more natural.

SARAH: Oh, I'm all in favour of the woman nipping behind a hedge, dropping her baby, and then rejoining the caravan two miles down the road, but unfortunately, these Hampstead type aborigines expect us to sterilise the hedge!

PHILIP: You exaggerate, Sarah.

SARAH: Only a little. I just wish that, instead of moving the hospital to Mrs Webster's house, Mrs Webster would just move to the hospital.

PHILIP: Where the baby can be induced to fit in with the midwives' tea-breaks.

SARAH: Could I have your car keys, Philip ...? My car's being serviced, you remember?

PHILIP: I've handed them back with the car.

SARAH: Oh no!

PHILIP: Of course ... After all the fond farewells, I wasn't going to go back to the office tomorrow just to leave them the car.

SARAH: Damn ... I'll have to get a taxi.

MARGERY: Take her, Jack ...

SARAH: There's no need ...

MARGERY: Look, Sarah, I didn't fix this. Mrs Webster has started her baby completely on her òwn.

SARAH: ... Jack?

[*They make for the door.*]

JACK: I won't be long.

[*They go out.*]

COLIN: I take it, Margery, you would have a marked aversion from a disinterested spectator, fascinated to see how you will handle this?

MARGERY: I'm afraid so, Colin.

COLIN: Yes, well. It was worth a try ... If you don't get anywhere with him, I'm in my bedroom.

[*He goes out.*]

PHILIP: What'll you drink?

MARGERY: Whisky.

[PHILIP *moves to the table.*]

What are you going to do?

PHILIP: I'm going away for a time ... I don't have any plans beyond that ...

MARGERY: No, you wouldn't, would you? Are you determined to go alone ...?

PHILIP: Sarah has her practice. She couldn't just up and leave.

MARGERY: I didn't mean that . . . and you know I didn't mean
that . . . I would like to come with you . . . I'm sorry. I
shouldn't have . . .

PHILIP: Why not? You ought to say what you want to say.

MARGERY: All right . . . I love you, Philip.

PHILIP: . . . I know . . . In a way, I love you too, but I don't
want to . . . lead you to . . . believe that we necessarily
have any future together . . .

MARGERY: I thought you had abandoned ideas of the future,
and wanted to live in the present . . .

PHILIP: Yes . . . but . . .

MARGERY: But nothing, Philip . . . I'm not asking for a cast-iron
money back guarantee that we'll walk arm in arm
into a silver-haired sunset.

PHILIP: But it's absurd, Margery. To escape from one
relationship that has failed to another that would
start with such tension and guilt.

MARGERY: You want everything, Philip. All the opposites at the
same time. You say you're against planning, but you
want to plan a relationship that will last.

PHILIP: No. That's not true. I don't want to pervert the
future, that's all. And you can do that just as easily by
destroying something in a minute, impulsively, as
by building something that will stay for years.

MARGERY: You want to conserve what's good.

PHILIP: I suppose so, Is that so bad?

MARGERY: On the face of it, no. But what's happened to our far-
seeing Socialist? The man who wanted to change the
bad old systems, to do away with tired old men.

PHILIP: Perhaps I've just become one of them.

MARGERY: Philip, you wouldn't *vote* Conservative, would you?

PHILIP: Of course I wouldn't. The Labour Party is conservative enough for me.

MARGERY: I'm sure Colin would welcome you to a party further
left.

PHILIP: But they're the most conservative of the lot. They quote statements made in 1848 as if they applied today. Like Lysenko's Marxist genetics; after they'd starved millions of peasants they had to concede that Lysenko couldn't get wheat to grow through the Siberian snow, but they've never really forgiven Nature for being so un-Marxist.

MARGERY: ... You're very clever, Philip. I told you I loved you, that I want to come away with you, and within two minutes we're talking politics.

PHILIP: ... Well ...

MARGERY: Why don't you say that you just don't want me enough ... ? It's perfectly simple.

PHILIP: Statements about attitudes that are perfectly simple are, by definition, perfectly wrong.

MARGERY: But you don't want me enough, do you?

PHILIP: I can't answer that question. It begs too many others. Want? In what way? For how long ... ? Enough? Of what? Sex? Companionship? Intellectual stimulation?

MARGERY: What do you want, for Christ's sake! Marilyn Monroe, Vanessa Redgrave, Germaine Greer, and your old mother, all rolled into one?

PHILIP: No ... I think my old mother would be acutely uncomfortable ... Sorry ... The only answer I can give you is that I don't know what I want. And I'm not likely to find out if I jump for the first solution that offers itself.

MARGERY: ... Well, Jack thinks I'm a problem. I suppose it's an advance to be thought of as a solution, even an inadequate one.

PHILIP: I don't want to hurt you Margery.

MARGERY: Philip?

PHILIP: ... Yes!

MARGERY: I have watched you fade away ... lose your nerve and

                I felt helpless because there's a barrier around you.
                Now if we could just give each other the time to be
                together, talk together, think together ... Can't I
                give you some of my energy? Vitality?

PHILIP: Yes.

MARGERY: Then take it, Philip ...

PHILIP: Margery, you are right. My nerve has gone. Perhaps
        the country's nerve has gone, I don't know. But our
        symptoms are the same. A loss of faith ... of
        appetite ... of restful sleep, even. All that may be
        true. But what do we do about it? Throw everything
        to the winds? Embark on a wild dash to freedom,
        kicking everything down in our path. I can't do it;
        perhaps that's another symptom of the disease. But
        ... there it is.

MARGERY: I'm not offering myself as a garment for ever, but as a
         woman who believes she could keep you warm now,
         but if the times change, might become ... un-
         necessary.

PHILIP: Oh, Margery! Do you think I could dispose of a
        human relationship, like an old coat?

MARGERY: But I would still like my frontage to finish up in
         your bedroom.

PHILIP: ... For that we'd need planning permission, and just
        at the moment, I don't think I could stand the public
        inquiry.

                [*He kisses* MARGERY *lightly and dis-
                engages himself. He moves to the drinks
                table and pours himself another drink.*]

        I'm sorry, Margery ...

                [*There is the sound of a car.*]

        That'll be Jack.

MARGERY: I ... I don't want to meet them ... I'll go out the back
         way ...

PHILIP: Please ...

MARGERY: I'm sorry, Philip, if I embarrass you . . . but . . .
[*She goes out the back way, through the kitchen.* JACK *and* SARAH *come in.*]

PHILIP: That was quick . . . False alarm . . . ?

SARAH: She hasn't had another contraction since she rang. In any case it'll be hours yet . . .

PHILIP: Oh . . .

JACK: Where's Margery?

PHILIP: She . . . she decided to go on home . . .

JACK: I see . . . Was she . . . upset?

PHILIP: She was very calm as she left . . . Just said she thought she'd go . . .

JACK: Well, perhaps I'd better follow her . . .

PHILIP: Oh, do stop for another drink, Jack . . . You wouldn't send me off stone cold sober, surely?

JACK: You want to give her time to recover herself, do you?

SARAH: Please Jack . . . Do have another drink . . .

JACK: All right, Sarah . . .

PHILIP: Good.
[PHILIP *pours.*]

SARAH: It *was* good of you to drive me, Jack . . .

JACK: It's nothing . . .

SARAH: I'll look in again before I go to bed, but I'm sure nothing will happen before tomorrow . . .
[PHILIP *gives* JACK *his drink.*]

PHILIP: There we are . . .

JACK: Thanks.

PHILIP: What about you, Sarah . . . ?

SARAH: I've still got mine here . . .

PHILIP: Right . . . Cheers . . .

JACK: I'm sorry, Philip . . . about that snide remark . . .

PHILIP: Forget it.

JACK: No. I'm sorry you had such a difficult time with Margery. I think you've behaved very well . . . you couldn't help it . . . if . . .

[*The kitchen door opens and* MARGERY *comes in.*]

MARGERY: If what? I'm sorry, Philip, for running away ... it seems so wet ... and, Jack, I'll do my own apologising if I think it's necessary. Now, where's my drink?

PHILIP: Coming.

MARGERY: Really, Sarah. I should be apologising to you, I suppose. I love Philip ... I begged him to take me with him ... He refused.

PHILIP: There's no need, Margery.

MARGERY: And I'll decide what I think I need to say ... I know, Sarah, you think I'm unbalanced ... or manic depressive, or some other jargon for batty, but if Philip were to send for me, I'd go.

SARAH: I shouldn't hold your breath while you wait ...

MARGERY: I shan't.

[PHILIP *hands her a drink.*]

Thank you ... Cheers.

PHILIP: Cheers.

[COLIN *comes back in.*]

COLIN: Is the party on again?

MARGERY: Yes. Come in. The irate husband has returned to punish his erring wife.

JACK: Why do you think it necessary to humiliate me in front of our friends ... ?

MARGERY: I don't. You humiliate yourself. You don't own me. If I go away, I take from you only what's mine. I don't diminish you. Unless, of course, you regard me as a possession.

PHILIP: Rubbish! Just now, you offered yourself to me as a cloak to keep me warm. If I accepted, and stood in the wind, and then you took it away, should I not freeze?

SARAH: ... As I shall.

PHILIP: . . . But this cloak is threadbare. You won't notice it's gone.

SARAH: Surely, Philip, that's for me to say.

PHILIP: Not necessarily. If the cloak is completely threadbare, it just falls off.

SARAH: No. I won't accept this tyranny of analogy. You are not a cloak, but a man, the father of our son, the joint owner of this house, and for twenty years, a sharer in my life . . . You are *not* a cloak. I am not a tailor's dummy.

PHILIP: No . . . Why is everything so demanding? Why do we crowd in on each other's lives, as though the very breath we breathe has to be taken from someone else's lungs?

SARAH: I don't think that's fair. You wanted the job here and you came. I followed. I've made my own life, worked and brought up Colin. I haven't made any demands. I've just admired what you've achieved . . . I still do — even though you've lost faith in it . . . I love you, and would like to come with you.

PHILIP: . . . I feel like a cross between Jack the Ripper and the Pied Piper of Hamelin . . . Why don't you come to Scarborough too, Jack? Then we can all build sand-castles together.

MARGERY: You haven't given up *all* thoughts of building, then, Philip?

PHILIP: I'll only build below the high-water mark . . .
[SARAH *makes to go.*]
I did hear you, Sarah. I'm sorry to have escaped into flippancy.

JACK: We ought to go.

PHILIP: Oh no, please. I don't want us all to slope off to our corners to lick our wounds. We've known each other for years, it's no way to part.

MARGERY: What do you suggest? Strip poker?

JACK: Colin, what did you think of your father's reading tonight?

COLIN: The Tower of Babel story? I thought it was marvellous.

PHILIP: Careful, Colin. Your comrades wouldn't be pleased.

COLIN: It just shows what an arrogant bugger God was. I mean, here we have some people taking their lives into their own hands, talking to each other, building, getting excited. Then along comes this old chap with a beard, kicks them in the arse, pulls down their tower, and mixes up their speech.

PHILIP: But the story is about pride . . .

COLIN: Right! About the pride in being a man! I mean, who is the pride dangerous to? Up till then, the old chap with the beard had had it all his own way, hadn't he? Builds himself a garden, puts a couple of plastic gnomes in it and kicks them out when they find a game he didn't like, and made it an extra-mural activity. When the gnomes got really independent, he drowned the lot, except for a few creeps who knew their place. Then, along comes another lot. "Right," they said, "let's build a tower; then we can go up and have it out with the old bugger, man to gnome." He wasn't going to stand for that, was he? How dare those gnomes get ideas above their station. They'd be designing their own garden next! And the one with the fishing rod will stroll over and look at the daffodils. And the one sitting on a mushroom will pick it and make soup. Chaos, anarchy!

PHILIP: But what if that tower they were building was a plutonium reactor? We know how to make one, we know how to use it, but there's hardly a leading politician in the world who doesn't wish the whole thing would just go away. In our pride and ignorance, we've already built ourselves towers, to the heaven, of unlimited power. Unfortunately, for us, your 'old chap with the beard' seems to have washed his hands of us, and won't come down any more to destroy the towers and confuse the scientific language so that the mistake can't be repeated.

[MARGERY *begins to cry quietly.*]

JACK: Margery?

PHILIP: I'll get you a brandy.

MARGERY: For God's sake ... Is that your cure for ... distress? To bludgeon it with words and if that fails, knock it out with alcohol.

JACK: Please, Margery.

MARGERY: No, I won't stop crying. That's what's needed here, isn't it? Some straight emotion, some honest-to-goodness tears if we can't manage some belly-splitting laughter.

PHILIP: I ... sorry, Margery ... I feel ...

MARGERY: No you don't. You bloody don't. That's what I'm saying. I look at you, and I can't see you. You're hiding behind a pile of words ... You're going away, and that wouldn't matter so much, if you'd ever really *been* here.

PHILIP: Oh, I've been here, all right ... I used to think it was only doctors who had monuments erected to their mistakes, but I've built a memorial to end all mausoleums.

MARGERY: Yes, you have! For the same reason. It doesn't laugh, it's merely witty.

PHILIP: You're right. It's urbane, not urban.

[MARGERY *looks at* PHILIP. *She is still sobbing. His remark frustrates her beyond reply. She goes to him and slaps him, hard.*]

JACK: Margery ...

[*He moves towards her. She swings round and freezes him with her look. She is tense and becomes icy cold.*]

MARGERY: [*to* SARAH] I expect you're working out how you can

71

get some Valium into me. [*to* JACK] And you're embarrassed because I'm making a scene . . . And what about you, Philip? Are you trying to work out how you can wittily turn the other cheek? If you do, I'll hit that too . . .

> [MARGERY *stops him again with her look.* *She turns to him and undoes her simple* *dress. It falls open. She is wearing nothing* *underneath.*]

What do you see, I'd like to know. We know about Sarah . . . She sees a female body with mammary glands and a pelvic girdle, adapted for childbearing. Jack sees a clothes-stand that, suitably draped, can really knock the eyes out of a Director of Education at the annual party . . . But you, what do you see . . . ? A 'frontage you don't want in your bedroom . . . ?' An example of dynamic design . . . ? Oh! Say you see a woman and we might have some hope . . .

PHILIP: . . . I'm sorry . . . I'm sorry, Margery.

> [MARGERY'*s energy slowly begins to drain.* COLIN *quickly steps to her. He takes her* *hand.*]

COLIN: I see a beautiful woman, with or without her clothes . . . But right now, I see somebody who . . . needs a cuddle.

> [MARGERY *melts on his shoulders and cries* *quietly.*]

And I also see somebody who doesn't know that the atmosphere in this house is so cold it's very dangerous not to be wrapped up warmly.

> [*He pulls her dress together. He holds her.*]

In fact, for really warm-blooded people, you can't survive here at all . . . so must come back next door.

> [*He leads her towards the door. Before they*

> *go out,* MARGERY *stops and looks back at* PHILIP.]

MARGERY: ... I pity you, Philip ... You can see so well ... You can see the woods, but you have to stand so far back, you can't hear the rustle of the leaves ... Goodbye.

> [*They go out.* JACK *follows.*]

SARAH: ... Perhaps you should have married somebody like that ...

PHILIP: No ... Perhaps I shouldn't have married anyone at all ... but if I did, it ought to have been someone who could resist me ... like you.

SARAH: ... That's true. But, it's hard, Philip. Very hard ... She was right, you know ... [*smiling*] about you, that is ... It's you that is so clinical. For someone so ... remote ... it is almost obscene that you should be so attractive.

> [COLIN *comes back.*]

COLIN: He almost snatched her ... I don't know what he thought I was going to do.

PHILIP: Thank you, Colin. You were ... magnificent.

COLIN: No Dad, just human ... but then, I suppose any cold-blooded animal must be amazed at the ability of a mammal to run about in the winter ... Goodnight.

> [*He makes to go.*]

PHILIP: Colin ... be careful ... To be able to deliver a shaft like that at a time like this, shows we are not *so* unalike ... Goodnight.

> [COLIN *goes out.*]

SARAH: Have you really no plans? It all seems so ... destructive.

PHILIP: I know ... but deep down in me ... somewhere ... I feel I'm doing the right thing.

SARAH: ... Will you try to get a job as an architect?

PHILIP: I have no plans ...

SARAH: You're not an adolescent setting off to hitch round Europe for two months knowing there's always somewhere safe to come back to.

PHILIP: I know. But middle age is what it says it is. The middle. It's not the end. When Abelard was castrated in middle age he . . .

SARAH: Philip! I don't want to hear about Abelard, or Stalin, or Socrates, or plutonium reactors. I want to hear about you . . . I'm your wife. I love you. I love you. We've built together a life, and it's been a good one for me, and I believe a productive one for you.

PHILIP: I've built my life like you build a motorway. You start at A and you crash through to B — the broad road to destruction. My life has been planning; so my life has been planned. It's time for listening to the small, still voice. It's time for some spontaneity.

SARAH: Yes, of course. But, can't you see, you are just as ruthlessly planning spontaneity. Pushing your road over Colin and me.

PHILIP: I know it must seem like that.

SARAH: It *is* like that.

PHILIP: Perhaps it is! But I have to do it. I have to get away.

SARAH: I shan't stop you . . . or do anything dramatic, like stripping off.

PHILIP: No . . . there you are . . . I did marry the right one.

SARAH: But did I . . . ? Just promise me one thing, Philip.

PHILIP: What's that?

SARAH: You're going tonight, aren't you? The eleven-fifteen train?

PHILIP: How did you know?

SARAH: I heard you make the phone call . . . Promise me that if you want to come back, if you ever get the feeling that you'd like me to be with you, you won't be too proud to come back.

PHILIP: I promise . . . but don't hold your breath, either.

74

SARAH: Goodbye Philip ... I'll go back to Mrs Webster. You'll be gone when I get back.
[*She kisses him lightly, and goes out.* PHILIP *goes to the phone and dials.*]

PHILIP: Could I have a taxi, please? Philip Turner ... here ... yes ... in half an hour ... thank you.
[*He replaces the phone. He looks around the room and then catches sight of the audience. He moves downstage. As he does so, the house lights come up.*]

PETER: Our play is over. I say 'our' because you've been quite a few characters — New Townsfolk, parents, teachers, pupils, members of an Historical Society, a congregation. And you've played them splendidly. To thank you, let me drop my character, and become again Peter Barkworth, to tell you, the audience in this theatre, a true story, found by our playwright who, somewhat ruefully, thinks it says just about as much as all his play put together. In 1492 the Borgia family celebrated the election of a Borgia pope by a marvellous pageant in Florence. One of the tableaux was of a fallen warrior in iron armour, and out of his back emerged a beautiful boy as Cupid, gilded to represent the new Golden Age arising out of the Iron ... It was most impressive and the innocence of the shining boy moved onlookers to tears. Two days later, the boy died from the effect of the gilding ...

Can you hear me at the back?

BLACKOUT

THE END

75

WHOSE LIFE IS IT ANYWAY?

Brian Clark

Ken Harrison lies in a hospital bed, paralysed from the neck down following a car crash. He faces the prospect of being totally dependent on a life-support machine, realising that even the final option of suicide can be denied him. "If you're clever and sane enough to put up an invincible case for suicide," he says, "it demonstrates you ought not to die."

"... a moving and absorbing drama about the struggle of a man for the right to die."

The Daily Telegraph

"Brian Clark has made a fascinating play out of this all too topical dilemma."

The Financial Times

THREE ONE-ACT PLAYS

Post Mortem   Brian Clark
Too Hot to Handle   Jim Hawkins
Sunbeams   Rosemary Mason

A collection of three modern comedies, each lasting 50-60 minutes in performance.

Post Mortem   Set in the modern office of a business tycoon. Helen Ansty, personal assistant to L.K. Halpin, arrives for work one morning unaware that her boss is dead. She takes over the running of the office for the day with remarkable results. — A strong leading female role plus 'voices on the phone' parts for 3-4 actors and one actress.

Too Hot to Handle   One day Suzanne discovers a cache of pornographic magazines in her husband's wardrobe. When he comes home from work that evening she confronts him with the evidence. — A domestic 'marriage-lines' comedy for two actresses and one actor.

Sunbeams   Set in London's bed-sit land. A social worker, Frances, meets Louise who runs a call-girl service from the flat upstairs. They begin to examine each other's role and function in society and realise that they are perhaps not so different after all. — A play for two actresses and one actor.

PIAF

Pam Gems

Pam Gems writes . . .

In the world of popular music, there are two giants and they are both women — Billie Holiday and Edith Piaf. Piaf, the street-waif, rickety, illegitimate, became the supreme mistress of the chanson, influencing and launching almost a whole generation of French singers. What was it about this small, dumpy woman in the plain black dress, looking like a concierge? How did she do it? In the first place she was, despite illness and personal tragedy, a supreme technician. But she was also a woman who never became inflated, never forgot her roots, and who never became involved with materialism. For her, singing was ecstasy. She believed above all in love, physical love. When she sang, she sang as a woman, as an adult. She sang of sexuality and, when the mood was sad, of betrayal: you believed her. She had been there. The accuracy and reality of her work is unique in a world usually characterised by the banal and the commercial. Miraculously, in a sentimental genre, Piaf found emotional truth. This was her genius.

"Quite stunning. A genuinely warm portrait of a woman who found relief from the frequent unhappiness in her life in the orgasmic joy of singing."

The Guardian

"Everything about the Piaf legend comes across with potent force."

Daily Mail